MASTERING A.I

A GUIDE TO UNDERSTANDING AND GROWING WITH GPT AND AI TECHNOLOGY.

Written By Sonyque Suriel

Copyright © 2024 Sonyque Suriel

All rights reserved

No part of this book may be reproduced, or stored in a retrieval system, or transmitted in any form or by any means, electronic, mechanical, photocopying, recording, or otherwise, without express written permission of the publisher.

ISBN: 9798340683229

Cover design by: Sonyque Suriel and DALL-E
Library of Congress Control Number: 2018675309
Printed in the United States of America

Disclaimer

The information provided in this book, "Mastering AI: A Guide to Understanding and Growing with ChatGPT and AI Technology," is for educational and informational purposes only. While every effort has been made to ensure the accuracy and completeness of the content, the author and publisher make no representations or warranties of any kind, express or implied, about the completeness, accuracy, reliability, suitability, or availability of the information contained in this book for any purpose.

The author and publisher shall not be liable for any errors or omissions in this information nor for any losses, injuries, or damages arising from its display or use. The use of AI technologies, including ChatGPT, involves complex algorithms and systems that may not always perform as expected. This book was written with the help of ChatGPT, so please fact-check all and any information.

The ethical implications of AI are significant and multifaceted. This book provides general guidance on ethical AI use, but it is not exhaustive. Readers are encouraged to stay informed about ongoing developments in AI ethics and to make decisions based on a thorough understanding of the potential impacts on society, individuals, and industries.

The content in this ebook is not intended to be a substitute for professional advice, financial, legal, or otherwise. Always seek the advice of a qualified professional with any questions you may have regarding a particular subject.

The field of AI is rapidly evolving. The author and publisher may update the content of this ebook as new information becomes available, but there is no obligation to do so. Readers are encouraged to seek out additional resources and stay informed about the latest developments in AI technology.

The author and publisher do not warrant or guarantee the

performance or reliability of AI tools and recommend that users exercise their judgment and discretion when implementing AI solutions. Any action you take upon the information in this book is strictly at your own risk.

CONTENTS

Mastering A.I	
Copyright	
Dedication:	1
Introduction:	2
What is a.i?	4
What is GPT?	8
GETTING STARTED WITH a.I:	12
a.i IN YOUR POCKET?	18
CAN A.I BE YOUR CREATIVE SIDEKICK?	22
a.I THERAPY	26
A.I AND PRIVACY	30
A.I FOR ENTREPRENEURS	35
A.I IN CAREERS	42
THE FUTURE OF A.I	47
The AI Journey Is Just Beginning	52
Acknowledgments	53
About The Author	55

DEDICATION:

To every curious soul, those who question, explore, and embrace the unknown with open minds. This book is for you. May it serve as a guide on your journey through the ever-evolving world of AI. To the Chosen Ones, my best friends and forever partners-in-adventure, thank you for always pushing me to discover more. Here's to our next adventure, maybe in code, maybe in the family. And most importantly to my mentor Sonalli Andrews and Redninko Designs, thank you for you patience and dedication to help me with this project.

INTRODUCTION:

Welcome to the World of AI

It's time to dive into a world that's not just a tech geek's playground but one that's rapidly becoming part of **all our** lives, Artificial Intelligence (AI). Whether you're just hearing about it or you've been around the block with GPT, chatbots, and smart devices, this book is for you.

AI isn't just some abstract, futuristic concept. It's right here, in your phone, your home, and even your favorite apps. It's helping you curate playlists, find the fastest route home, and maybe even cure diseases. But there's more to it than that, and that's where this guide comes in.

In this book, we're not just going to talk about AI, we're going to understand it, get comfortable with it, and figure out how to make it work for *you*. Whether you're looking to boost your career, improve your self-care routine, or tap into new business ideas, AI has something to offer you. And trust me, it's not as complicated as it sounds. Think of AI as your personal assistant, therapist, creative buddy, or even your entrepreneurial sidekick, there to make your life easier, not take it over.

So, let's take a deep breath, shake off any fears or uncertainties, and step into the world of AI together. You're about to learn how this tech can empower you, and maybe even surprise you along the way. Let's go!

Understanding AI is Becoming Universally Valuable.

WHAT IS A.I?

(In a way that *actually* makes sense)

So, let's start at the beginning. What *is* Artificial Intelligence (AI)? If you're thinking, "robots, self-driving cars, maybe that creepy AI from every sci-fi movie," you're not *wrong*, but there's a lot more to it. AI is basically about teaching machines to *think*, or at least, mimic human thought in a way that helps us solve problems, automate tasks, and make our lives easier.

AI: The Brainy, Non-Human Helper

In its simplest form, AI refers to the simulation of human intelligence by machines. Now, that's a lot of words, but here's what it boils down to: imagine a machine, like your computer, *learning* to do things humans typically do, like understanding language, recognizing patterns, making decisions, and even learning from mistakes.

At its core, AI is about taking tasks that require thinking and handing them over to computers, so they can do it faster and, sometimes better than we can. Whether it's recommending what movie you should watch next on Netflix or figuring out how to route delivery trucks most efficiently, AI is the secret sauce behind the scenes making all of this happen.

So, How does AI work?

Think of AI as having two big brains. One brain is the "rule-following" brain, where the computer follows a set of instructions humans give, like a recipe. This is often referred to as *narrow AI* or *weak AI* (don't let the names fool you, though, it's still powerful).

The other brain is where AI *learns*, this is called *machine learning*, and it's like AI figuring out things on its own by looking at data, making predictions, and getting better over time. It's like the AI version of "practice makes perfect."

In practice, this learning means that AI doesn't need to be programmed for every single scenario. Let's say you have an AI that's learning to recognize pictures of cats. Instead of telling it, "Hey, this is a cat!" For every single image, you show it thousands of images, and over time, it figures out the patterns, cats have whiskers, they're usually fluffy, they have pointy ears and they start recognizing cats on their own. It's the ultimate study buddy, except it never gets tired or distracted.

Types of AI: From Your Phone to Science Fiction

Not all AI is built the same, so let's break it down:

1. **Narrow AI**: This is the AI you already interact with daily. Think Siri, Alexa, Netflix recommendations, or those chatbots that pop up on websites. Narrow AI is designed to do specific tasks, it knows its lane and stays in it. Whether that's recognizing speech, recommending songs, or playing chess at a world-champion level. It can't do *everything*, but it can absolutely crush that one thing it's built for.
2. **General AI**: This is the kind of AI you see in movies, a system that can do *anything* a human can. Think of Jarvis from *Iron Man* or HAL from *2001: A Space Odyssey*. We're not there yet. General AI would mean machines have the ability to reason, learn, and apply that learning across all different areas of life, basically making them as smart as, or smarter than, humans.
3. **Superintelligence**: Now, this is where things get sci-fi-level scary. Superintelligence refers to AI that is way beyond human intelligence like Einstein times a million. But here's the thing: we're nowhere near that.

Right now, AI can't even pass for a convincing human in most conversations. So, let's put our fears about superintelligent overlords on pause for now.

How AI Learns (The "Training" Part)

So how does AI get so smart? It's all about data. AI learns by being fed a *ton* of data, just like when we learn by practicing over and over again. Whether it's recognizing cats or driving a car, AI gets better by seeing more examples and understanding patterns. This is what's called *machine learning*, where the AI trains on data and improves its performance over time.

Then there's something called *deep learning*, which is a type of machine learning that's modeled after the human brain. It's about building neural networks, systems of algorithms that help the AI learn more complex tasks, like understanding language or recognizing images. Deep learning is why AI can now write, draw, and even make music!

Let me explain Automation

Automation is like handing off your most repetitive, time-consuming tasks to a super-efficient digital assistant that never gets tired. It's about using technology to streamline processes, whether it's sending emails, managing inventory, or even responding to customers, so you can focus on what really matters. Instead of doing the grunt work yourself, automation takes care of it in the background, making your workflow smoother and your life way easier.

Why AI Matters to You

I'm not going to wait until the end of the book to give you the secret, so here it is. AI isn't just about futuristic tech; it's already here, shaping the way we live, work, and play. And as we move forward, it's only going to get more integrated into our lives. Whether you're a business owner looking to streamline processes or just someone who wants their playlist recommendations to be just a little better, AI is working for you behind the scenes.

WHAT IS GPT?

To move forward you have to know GPT. So, you've probably heard the term "GPT" tossed around a lot lately. Maybe you've even used it without really knowing what it is. At its core, GPT is an AI model designed to understand and generate human-like text. It belongs to a class of AI models known as Transformers, which have revolutionized how we handle natural language processing (NLP). Developed by OpenAI, GPT is trained on a massive amount of text data to learn patterns in language, enabling it to respond to text prompts intelligently and generate new content.

GPT: The Breakdown

First things first: GPT stands for **Generative Pre-trained Transformer**. Sounds fancy, right? Well, it is. But let's strip away the tech jargon and get to what that really means for you.

- **Generative**: This means that GPT can *create* stuff, like text, stories, poems, or even code based on the information it's been trained on. It's like a content wizard that can write anything from an email to a Shakespearean sonnet (or at least try).
- **Pre-trained**: This is important. GPT has been trained on *massive* amounts of text data like everything from books and websites to academic papers. The "pre-trained" part means it already knows a lot, so you don't have to start from scratch. It's like buying a smartphone that's already loaded with apps, ready to go.
- **Transformer**: No, it's not Optimus Prime. The "transformer" here is the model's architecture basically, the brain that helps GPT understand the relationships between words and

generate coherent responses.

In short, GPT is your all-knowing, super-efficient assistant who can write, explain, and *create* content based on anything you ask for. You give it a prompt, it gives you back results that feel like magic.

Why GPT Feels Human-ish (But Isn't)

The reason GPT feels like it's having a real conversation with you is because of how it's built. It's trained to understand patterns in language, like how certain words go together, what a question looks like, and how to respond based on context. It's why GPT can answer, "How's the weather?" with, "It's sunny in New York today!" even though it doesn't actually *know* what the weather is (it's pulling info from its training data). Think of GPT as that one friend who always knows what you're about to say next. It predicts the next word in a sentence based on what you've already typed, kind of like finishing each other's sentences, but without the awkwardness!

However, it's important to remember GPT doesn't "think" like we do. It doesn't have feelings or intentions. It's not sentient. It's just really good at sounding like it understands you because of how much data it's been trained on.

GPT in Action

Here's where things get cool. GPT can do way more than just answer your questions, it can help you *create* in ways you've probably never imagined. Here's a quick rundown of how you can use GPT:

1. **Writing Assistant**: Need help drafting an email, writing a report, or brainstorming ideas? GPT's got your back. Just ask it to help you, and it'll generate content that's clear, structured, and tailored to your needs.
2. **Language Tutor**: Want to brush up on your Spanish or French? GPT can explain grammar rules, help you

practice vocabulary, and even hold a basic conversation in another language.
3. **Coding Companion**: If you're into coding (or trying to learn), GPT can help you write and debug code. Just ask it for help with Python, JavaScript, or whatever language you're working with.
4. **Personal Researcher**: Need to understand a new concept or look up a fact? GPT is like Google, but it gives you more conversational answers instead of just spitting out links.
5. **Creative Brainstormer**: Struggling with a creative block? Ask GPT for ideas, whether you're writing a novel, starting a business, or creating content. It's like having a second brain to bounce ideas off of.

Real-Life Scenarios

Here are five ways you can put GPT to work *right now* in your everyday life:

- **Career Hacks**: Let's say you're prepping for a job interview. GPT can generate potential interview questions, help you practice your answers, and even give feedback on your resume or LinkedIn profile.
- **Content Creation**: Imagine you're running a blog or social media account. Need help writing captions, coming up with hashtags, or planning your next post? GPT can help with that. Ask it to give you creative ideas or edit your draft for clarity.
- **Learning New Skills**: Let's say you want to learn about investing in the stock market but don't know where to start. Ask GPT for a beginner's guide to investing, and it'll break down complicated terms in a way that actually makes sense.
- **Customer Service**: Running a small business? GPT can help you draft polite, professional responses to customer inquiries or complaints, saving you tons of time.
- **Home Projects**: Thinking of redecorating or working on

a DIY project? Ask GPT for ideas on color schemes, budget-friendly materials, or even step-by-step instructions for building a bookshelf. It's like having a personal handyman, minus the actual hands.

Tips for Getting the Most Out of GPT

- **Be Clear with Your Prompts**: The better your question, the better the answer. If you're vague, GPT might give you a generic response. But if you're specific, like, "Write me a 300-word blog post on the benefits of meditation" you'll get exactly what you need.
- **Iterate and Refine**: GPT is great, but it's not perfect. If it doesn't give you what you want on the first try, tweak your prompt or ask for clarification. It learns from how you interact with it.
- **Experiment**: Don't be afraid to ask GPT for offbeat stuff. Whether it's coming up with recipes, writing poems, or brainstorming a business plan, GPT is flexible. Use it creatively and push the limits.

What's Next for GPT?

As we move into the future, GPT is only going to get better. With each new version, the model learns more, gets more efficient, and becomes better at understanding context and nuance. The goal is to make AI as helpful as possible in our daily lives, making things easier, faster, and more productive for us.

GETTING STARTED WITH A.I:

If you've never used GPT or any form of AI, don't worry, it's not as intimidating as it sounds. Think of it as chatting with an extremely knowledgeable friend who's always ready to help.

Start with Curiosity

You're typing questions or prompts, and instead of showing you links, GPT gives you direct answers, explanations, or even creative outputs, like poems or stories. Start by asking simple questions like:

- "What are some fun facts about Japan?"
- "Can you explain how the stock market works in simple terms?"

It's All About Prompts

A "prompt" is just what you ask GPT to do. Your prompt could be a question, a request for advice, or even something creative. The clearer and more specific your prompt, the better the response. For example:

- Vague: "Tell me about food."
- Specific: "What are some popular traditional foods in Scotland and how are they made?"

To get the most out of ChatGPT and receive more personalized responses, it's key to incorporate yourself into the prompts. Why? Because when you add your voice, context, and personal style, the ai can tailor its suggestions to fit your needs, vibe, and audience.

For example, instead of asking, "Write a caption for my business," try something like, "I want a fun, light-hearted caption for my press-on nail business with a sunny, happy vibe. What should I say?" This way, the responses align with your brand's personality, making it feel more authentic and true to you.

It's all about helping ChatGPT "get to know" your tone, your audience, and what makes your message unique!

The more details you add, the better your experience will be!

Don't Worry About Being Formal

When using GPT, you don't need to be super technical. Just type naturally, as if you're talking to a person. You can be casual, direct, or even playful. You can say:

- "Hey, can you help me plan a workout routine?"
- "I need some inspiration for a story about a detective. Can you brainstorm ideas?"

It's all about experimenting and finding the tone that feels right for you.

Try Out Different Uses

AI can help in various ways depending on what you're into. Whether you're writing, learning, planning, or just curious, there's something for everyone. Here are a few ways you can explore:

- **Content Creation**: "Can you write a blog post on self-care tips for beginners?"
- **Learning**: "Explain quantum physics in a way a 5th grader would understand."
- **Daily Planning**: "Help me organize my weekly to-do list."
- **Cooking**: "Give me a quick and easy recipe for dinner tonight."

Experiment with Conversations

If the first response isn't quite what you wanted, don't be shy to tweak your prompt and ask it again. For example:

- "Tell me more about that" if you want a deeper explanation.
- "Summarize that in a sentence" if you're short on time.

Feel free to play around and discover the best way it can help you!

Use GPT Creatively

AI can go beyond just giving factual answers. It can brainstorm, generate ideas, or even write fiction. Here's where it gets fun:

- **Story Writing**: Ask GPT to write the beginning of a short story, then continue it yourself.
- **Inspiration**: "Give me 5 business ideas based on my interest in fitness."
- **Problem Solving**: "What are some unique ways to save money on groceries?"

When using AI, like ChatGPT, it's important to be minful of plagiarism and ethics. AI generates responses based on patterns in the data it's been trained on, which means it pulls from a vast amount of existing content. To avoid plagiarism, you should always tweak and personalize the AI's output. Use it as a starting point, but make sure your work reflects your voice and perspective. Adding personal experiences, insights, or examples makes your content unique. Ethically, it's key to credit sources, and not pass off AI-generated text as entirely your own.

By injecting your own creativity and authenticity, you'll produce original work that stands out while staying ethical

Make It Part of Your Routine

The great thing about AI is how you can make it part of your daily life. Need a quick decision? Want to learn something new? Stuck with a creative block? GPT has your back. It's like having a coach, teacher, and creative partner all in one.

Best Practices

- **Start Small**: If you're overwhelmed, start with basic questions. Once you're comfortable, you can explore more complex prompts.
- **Stay Curious**: The more you ask, the more you'll learn. GPT works best when you're engaged and curious.
- **Check for Accuracy**: While GPT is really smart, it's not perfect. Always double-check facts, especially if you're using AI for important decisions or tasks.

Real-World Examples

For Resumes:

- "Help me write a resume for a [specific job] position with [X] years of experience."

- "What are some strong action verbs I can use to describe my work experience in [industry]?"

- "Can you give me a bullet-point summary for my experience in [job title] at [company]?"

- "How can I format a resume to highlight my skills over my job experience?"

- "What keywords should I include in my resume for a [job role] to pass an ATS system?"

For Essays:

- "Outline an essay on [topic], including an introduction, thesis, body paragraphs, and conclusion."

- "Give me 3 arguments for and 3 against [debate topic] to use in my essay."

- "Can you help me rewrite my essay introduction to make it more engaging?"

- "Explain [specific concept] in simple terms for an essay on [topic]."

- "How do I structure a persuasive essay on [topic] with evidence and counterarguments?"

For Homework:

- "Explain the key points of [topic] in 200 words for a homework summary."

- "What are 5 important facts about [historical event/scientific concept] I should include in my homework?"

- "Can you walk me through solving this math problem: [insert problem]?"

- "What are the main themes of [book or story] that I can use for my homework?"

- "How can I compare and contrast [two topics] in a homework assignment?"

Remember, when using ChatGPT to teach you something, get specific with your prompts. For example, ask, "Explain the basics of aeronautical engineering like I'm a beginner, but keep it simple." If you want to be quizzed, you can prompt it with, "Quiz me on aeronautical engineering concepts and give me hints before revealing the answers." This way, you get a challenge while learning. For deeper understanding, try asking, "Can you explain where I went wrong in this answer and how I can improve?" This method helps ChatGPT guide you step by step while adjusting based on your understanding.

Here are some other practical ways you could use GPT in your daily life:

1. **Planning a Trip**: "Can you help me create a 5-day itinerary for India during Diwali season?"
2. **Learning a New Skill**: "Explain the basics of investing in

government bonds."
3. **Creative Writing**: "Give me a unique plot twist for my detective novel."
4. **Budgeting**: "Help me create a monthly budget for someone who earns $24,000 a year."
5. **Work Tasks**: "Write a professional email response to a client asking for a project update."

Getting started with GPT is all about being open, experimenting, and having fun with it. You can ask it anything, and the more you play around, the better you'll get at using AI to improve your day-to-day life.

A.I IN YOUR POCKET?

You're Already an AI User, Surprise! I'll be showing you how AI is already woven into our everyday lives, most of us don't even notice. You're already using it, and it's making life easier, smarter, and more fun.

We're living in a time where AI is casually hanging out on our phones, our laptops, and even in our smartwatches and we don't even realize it. When we're swiping through social media, streaming our favorite music, or chatting with a virtual assistant, AI is right there, doing its thing. Think of it like a quiet little helper who's always working in the background, making suggestions, optimizing, and giving you what you want (even before you know you want it).

Let's break down where AI is hiding in plain sight, right in your pocket.

Your Digital Butlers

You've probably talked to Siri, Google Assistant, or Alexa at some point, right? These virtual assistants are classic examples of AI at work. They recognize your voice, understand your commands, and fetch answers from the web faster than you can say "Where's my coffee?" AI powers these assistants to learn from your habits whether you're asking for directions, setting alarms, or just having them play your favorite tunes.

Imagine saying, "Alex, add cat food to my cart?" and boom! You're ready to check out your cart. But it's more than just that, these assistants remember things. They get to know your preferences over time, like when you usually leave for work, so they might suggest leaving earlier if there's traffic.

AI Behind Your Camera Roll

Now, let's talk about your photos. Ever noticed how your phone can automatically sort your pictures into albums of people, places, or even events? That's AI, Apps like Google Photos and Apple Photos use image recognition to categorize your snapshots, no tagging is required. It knows when you upload a photo, and it automatically recognizes who's in it. That's AI scanning faces, learning patterns, and then telling you, "Hey, that's your friend from last weekend's beach trip." It doesn't just stop there; some apps like FaceApp or Snapchat use AI to apply filters or even age you into the future!

Music and Movie Recommendations

Let's move on to the streaming world. Whether you're a Spotify addict or bingeing the latest show on Netflix, AI is all over that, too. Ever wondered how Spotify seems to magically know what songs to suggest next in your playlist? Or how Netflix seems to read your mind and just put that perfect new series right on your homepage? Yup, that's AI again!

AI analyzes your listening and viewing habits, what you skip, what you replay, and what you watch for hours (hello, guilty pleasures) and builds a pattern to recommend things you'll love. So when you find yourself on a never-ending binge of shows that are way too similar, blame the AI that's nailed down your taste.

AI on Social Media (The Algorithm Knows All)

Then, of course, there's social media. Whether you're on Instagram, TikTok, or Facebook, AI is what's showing you content you're most likely to engage with. Every like, comment, or share tells the AI something about what you're into. Suddenly, your feed is flooded with cat memes (because you "liked" one), DIY home improvement videos, or that weird but interesting corner of the internet dedicated to rare plants.

AI takes all of this data and tweaks your experience so it's personalized just for you. Your feed is being built in real-time, evolving with every scroll. TikTok's AI is particularly famous (or infamous) for being scarily accurate at knowing exactly what will hook you next.

AI and Smart Shopping

Ever notice how Amazon knows what you might want before you even know? That's AI looking at your past purchases, and items you've viewed, and comparing you to millions of other shoppers to predict what you might be interested in next. It's the same on fashion apps, grocery shopping, or even when booking flights or hotels.

AI is the invisible shopping assistant who's always whispering, "Hey, how about adding this to your cart?" And while it can sometimes feel like the algorithm knows a little too much about you, it's also super convenient when it suggests something you might actually need (or that perfect birthday gift for your bestie).

Health and Fitness

Don't forget about those AI-powered fitness apps like Fitbit, MyFitnessPal, or Apple Health. They're tracking your steps, monitoring your heart rate, and even recommending workouts based on your data. Whether you're into tracking your sleep patterns or crushing your daily step goals, these apps use AI to give you insights that help you hit your health targets.

Say you've been walking more than usual, your fitness app might congratulate you and nudge you to keep the streak alive. And those smartwatches? They're basically mini-AI health coaches, keeping you accountable without ever needing to set foot in the gym.

So, the next time someone tells you AI is just "futuristic tech," you can laugh, knowing that it's already running half of the apps you use daily. AI is in your pocket, quietly enhancing your life, and making things easier, faster, and smarter. But now that you know about it, you can start using it with purpose! Don't just let the AI make decisions for you, take control and figure out how to make it work with you in ways you didn't even realize were possible.

CAN A.I BE YOUR CREATIVE SIDEKICK?

I bet you knew this, but AI can help unleash that inner creative genius! Whether you're an artist, writer, entrepreneur, or just someone who loves dabbling in new ideas. Spoiler alert: AI isn't here to replace your creative spark; it's here to *amplify* it.

Creativity + AI = Magic

When you think about AI, creativity might not be the first thing that comes to mind. But trust me, AI and creativity go together like Sushi and Soy Sauce. AI is like having a 24/7 brainstorming buddy who's always ready to throw ideas at you, assist with designs, generate concepts, or even help you outline your next big project.

From generating artwork to writing the first draft of your novel, AI can *inspire* you, but it won't steal your show. It's the tool that works alongside your creativity, not a replacement for it.

Design and Art

If you're into visual arts, apps like **DALL·E** and **MidJourney** are perfect examples of how AI can get those creative juices flowing. These tools let you describe a concept or idea, and just like that! You get a generated piece of art. Think of it as a way to visualize ideas that are floating around in your head but haven't quite formed into something concrete yet.

Imagine you're designing a logo for your new brand but just can't decide on the style. You can use AI-powered design tools to create quick mock-ups. These aren't just cookie-cutter templates, either. AI tools can generate fresh, custom designs based on the parameters you set.

This doesn't mean AI does all the work for you, far from it! You'll still tweak, refine, and polish your creations. But AI helps cut down the time it takes to get from a *vague idea* to a *visual masterpiece*.

Writing and Storytelling

Let's say you've got an idea for a book, blog post, or even social media content, but you're struggling with writer's block. AI can help! Tools like **ChatGPT**, **Jasper AI**, and **Sudo Write** can assist in drafting, structuring, and even editing your written work.

Need help with dialogue for your characters? Ask the AI to come up with a conversation between a pirate and a detective, it'll give you a fresh angle to build on. Want to brainstorm some catchy taglines for your new product? AI can whip up a list of ideas for you to refine.

Of course, you'll still have to bring your own *voice* and *vision* to the table, but having AI as a creative partner means you can spend less time staring at a blank page and more time crafting something you're truly proud of.

Music and Sound

Got a tune in your head but don't know how to translate it into a full track? AI can help with that too. Apps like **Amper Music** or **Aiva** allow you to create custom tracks by selecting genres, instruments, and moods, and they'll do the heavy lifting for you. Whether you need background music for a YouTube video or you're composing an entire album, AI gives you a platform to experiment with sound.

And hey, it's not just music. AI is also used in sound editing for podcasts, audio effects, and even film scores. AI can analyze audio patterns, suggest the best transitions, or adjust the tempo, so your final product is clean and polished.

Content Creation for Entrepreneurs

If you're a business owner or an entrepreneur, AI can be your secret weapon for creating engaging content. Platforms like **Canva** now incorporate AI to help design professional-looking graphics, infographics, and social media posts in no time. No design degree required!

Let's just say you need a series of Instagram posts to promote a new product launch. You can describe the theme to AI-powered design tools, and in minutes, you'll have templates, colors, and layout suggestions ready to go. It's acts like a full creative team at your fingertips without the overhead cost.

And don't forget about **marketing copy**. AI can help you draft emails, ad copy, and blog posts, so you're not spending hours trying to figure out how to communicate your message. Instead, AI handles the heavy lifting, and you focus on making sure it speaks in your brand's unique voice.

Collaborate, Don't Delegate

Here's the key takeaway: AI is not here to take over your creativity, it's here to enhance it. It's the perfect sidekick: supportive, ready to assist, but it knows you're the hero of the story. You're the one calling the shots, deciding what works and what doesn't.

For example, if you're designing a website, AI can help with layout suggestions or content blocks. But at the end of the day, you'll be the one deciding what fits your vision and brand.

Real-World Example: Content Creators Using AI

Let's say you're a YouTuber creating content around fashion. You can use AI to help with video editing by automatically cutting boring segments, enhancing visuals, or even creating captions in different languages. Tools like **Descript** use AI to transcribe your videos and offer quick, intelligent editing options. The AI saves you time, but you're still the one deciding what makes the final cut.

Another example? **BuzzFeed** and **The New York Times** have already started using AI to help generate article ideas or fill in content gaps. It's not writing the entire article, it's giving the writers a head start by handling the more tedious tasks, like keyword analysis or formatting.

AI as Your Creative Partner

The bottom line is that AI can make your work more efficient, polished, and (let's be real) fun. Whether you're brainstorming ideas, generating visuals, composing music, or writing the next bestseller, AI is there to help you bring your vision to life. So, go ahead and give it a shot!. Who knows what genius you'll unleash with a little digital help?

A.I THERAPY

AI as Your Digital Therapist (SORT OF)

Alright, let's get real for a second. We all have days when life just feels *heavy*. Whether it's stress from work, personal life, or just feeling down, we could all use some support. But not everyone has access to therapy or mental health professionals when they need it. This is where AI steps in, offering a bridge between those rough moments and professional care.

Now, I'm not saying AI can replace a therapist, that's definitely not the goal, but AI apps like **Woebot** and **Wysa** have been designed to provide some level of emotional support. Think of them as those friends who always check in on you, making sure you're okay, and offering suggestions when you're feeling overwhelmed. These AI tools are rooted in cognitive behavioral therapy (CBT) techniques, meaning they can help guide you through some basic self-help strategies like journaling, mindfulness, and reframing negative thoughts.

For example, Woebot will ask how you're doing, suggest some positive activities if you're feeling down, and provide guidance on how to manage anxiety.

Meditation and Mindfulness Made Easy

Ever tried meditating on your own and found your mind wandering after two minutes? Same. That's why AI-powered meditation apps like **Headspace** and **Calm** are a total game-changer. These apps don't just throw a bunch of random meditations at you; they're smart enough to personalize your sessions based on how you're feeling, your schedule, and even your goals.

With AI learning your preferences, it'll recommend a quick 5-minute breathing exercise when you're short on time, or suggest a full 30-minute relaxation session if you've had a stressful day. They can even track your progress, nudging you when it's time to check in again.

Sleep Like a Baby (With AI's Help)

If you're like most of us, sleep doesn't always come easy. But guess what? AI is all over this too. Apps like **Sleep Cycle** and **Pzizz** use AI to analyze your sleep patterns and help you improve your rest. Sleep Cycle monitors your movements and sounds while you sleep, giving you feedback on how well you're sleeping and even waking you up at the optimal time so you feel more refreshed. (Yes, there's a science to waking up feeling good, and AI has figured it out!)

Pzizz goes a step further by combining AI with neuroscience to generate personalized sleep sounds and relaxation techniques. Whether you need to wind down before bed or power through a midday nap, AI is there to guide you into a peaceful slumber.

AI Reminders for Your Mental Wellness

It's easy to forget self-care when you're caught up in the hustle, but AI has your back. Apps like **Youper** and **Sanvello** provide daily mood tracking and check-ins, helping you stay on top of your mental health over time. These apps use AI to analyze patterns in your mood and suggest helpful content, coping mechanisms, or exercises based on how you've been feeling.

So, if the app notices that your mood dips around certain times or after specific activities, it'll remind you to take a break, practice gratitude, or engage in some relaxation techniques. It gives a little nudge to remind you to put *yourself* first, even if it's just for five minutes.

AI and Virtual Support Communities

Sometimes, we just need to talk to *some(body)* who gets it. AI has made it easier to find supportive communities where you can share your experiences and learn from others. Platforms like **Koko** use AI to moderate online support groups, ensuring that the conversations stay positive and productive while giving users the chance to connect with people going through similar challenges.

In these communities, AI helps to filter out negative or harmful content, making sure the space is safe and supportive for everyone. So while you're still connecting with real people, AI is there in the background, keeping things uplifting and constructive.

Real-World Example: Youper

Youper, for example. Youper is an AI-powered mental health assistant that uses your conversations with it to help track your mood, offer personalized insights, and suggest coping mechanisms. It's not about giving you generic advice; Youper adapts to your emotional state over time and can even recommend when you might want to consider talking to a professional.

So, whether you're feeling anxious, overwhelmed, or just a little off, Youper kind of always knows when something's up and gives you a gentle nudge in the right direction.

AI for Self-Care!

The beauty of using AI for mental health and self-care is that it's *always there*. You don't need to wait for an appointment, and you don't have to explain your life story every single time. AI can pick up on patterns, analyze your behaviors, and offer real-time, personalized suggestions to help you with whatever, whether that's a quick breathing exercise, a guided meditation, or even a vent session.

And *remember*, **AI isn't meant to replace traditional therapy**

or professional help. It's simply another tool in your self-care arsenal, giving you more ways to manage your mental health on a daily basis.

AI for self-care isn't some futuristic concept, it's already here, and it's ready to help you take care of yourself in ways that are smart, convenient, and effective. Whether you need a mental break, help with sleeping, or just a mood check, AI-powered tools can guide you toward better mental health.

But remember, just like any self-care tool, AI is *your* partner, not your savior. It's there to assist, not to replace the deeper support you might need from people in your life or mental health professionals. It's one piece of a much bigger puzzle, and when used right, it can make a huge difference in your overall wellness.

A.I AND PRIVACY

We're going to break down the big questions around privacy, making it practical and less scary, but real.

AI and Your Privacy

We've all had those moments: you're talking about something random, like how much you want to experience Mardi Gras, and then boom! Next time you check your phone, there's an ad for flights to New Orleans. It's like your devices are reading your mind. This, my friend, is the magic and mystery of AI. But before we start thinking it's all about conspiracy theories, let's get into the nitty-gritty of how AI interacts with our privacy.

AI lives and breathes data. It's kind of like a digital Sherlock Holmes, picking up clues about your likes, habits, and preferences to give you the best experience possible. But sometimes, Sherlock gets a bit too nosey, and that's where privacy concerns come in. How much of *you* is too much to share? And how do you make sure your data is used to make your life better, not leave you feeling exposed?

The Trade-off: Convenience vs. Privacy

Let's face it, we love convenience. AI can order our food, suggest the best music for our mood, or even recommend the perfect outfit based on the weather. But that convenience comes with a cost: *data*. When we use AI-driven services, we're often giving away more information than we realize. Think about every app you use. From location services to browsing habits(which is just *cookies*), a lot of our data is being collected behind the scenes to create those seamless, personalized experiences we've come to expect.

This doesn't mean we need to panic and delete everything, but it does mean we need to be aware of what we're sharing. It's a balancing act: How much info are you comfortable giving up to get the convenience you want?

Data Collection: What Exactly Are They Collecting?

Okay, so what kind of data are we talking about? The most common types of AI systems include:

- **Location data:** Ever notice how your phone suggests nearby restaurants or the quickest route home? That's your location data at work.
- **Browsing history:** Those targeted ads? That's your browser activity being analyzed.
- **Interactions and preferences:** AI can remember the things you like, the videos you watch, and the way you interact with certain apps or websites.

All this data allows AI to "learn" and improve its responses, but if it falls into the wrong hands, it can feel so invasive. So, it's crucial to understand how to manage these settings and protect your info.

How to Protect Your Privacy in an AI-Driven World

Now that we know what's at stake, let's talk about how to take control of your privacy while still enjoying the perks of AI.

1. Check Your Privacy Settings

This one's huge. Whether it's on your phone, your social media apps, or your AI devices like Alexa or Siri, privacy settings are your first line of defense. Most apps let you control what data they collect. Get into the habit of regularly reviewing and updating those settings. Turn off things you don't need, like location services for certain apps that have no business knowing where you are.

2. Be Mindful of What You Share

Before hitting "accept" on those terms of service agreements (we've all done it without reading), pause for a second. Ask yourself what you're agreeing to. Sometimes it's worth saying no if it feels like they're asking for too much access to your personal life. Do you really need an app tracking your location 24/7? Probably not.

3. Use Encrypted Tools

If you're using apps that handle sensitive information like financial or health-related ones make sure they use encryption. Encryption helps to secure your data from hackers or unauthorized access. Services like WhatsApp and Signal are good examples of encrypted messaging apps.

4. Read Up on Data Breaches

This one might sound a bit much, but stay informed. If a company has been involved in a data breach, it's good to know. You might want to change your passwords, use two-factor authentication, or limit your interactions with that service.

AI's Responsibility in Protecting Your Data

AI companies have a responsibility to keep your data safe. Many are now implementing things like "data anonymization," which means even if they collect your info, it's stripped of anything personal that could directly link it back to you. Another thing you'll hear about is **"differential privacy."** This basically means AI models can learn from data without accessing your personal details, keeping your private stuff private.

Companies are also leaning into transparency. Some are even creating what we could call **"data transparency reports"** (receipts) that tell you exactly what data they're collecting and how they're using it.

Real-Life Example: Google and Your Privacy

Google is a massive player in the AI game. It collects tons of data through services like Google Maps, Gmail, and YouTube. To its credit, Google gives you control over how much data it collects via the **Google My Activity** dashboard. Here, you can review, pause, or delete your search history, location tracking, and app activity. It's a way to be more proactive about what you're sharing and take back some control over your privacy.

AI and Data Breaches

Data breaches are the stuff of nightmares, and when AI systems are involved, the scale of the problem can be even bigger. Imagine a system that collects data from millions of people, if that data gets compromised, it's a huge deal. Just think about the **Equifax breach** in 2017, where millions of people's personal information was leaked.

While AI itself isn't the villain here, it often holds the keys to *a lot* of sensitive data. If that data gets compromised, it's not just a tech issue—it's a breach of trust. Companies need to seriously step up their security game with AI systems, from encrypting data to controlling access. Accountability isn't optional

Where Do We Go From Here?

Looking ahead, AI and privacy are going to be hot topics. As AI becomes smarter and more integrated into our lives, it will also need to become more transparent and secure. Governments are stepping in with new regulations, like the **General Data Protection Regulation (GDPR)** in Europe, which sets some strict rules about how companies can collect and use personal data.

More importantly, though, it's going to be up to us, the users, to stay informed and make smart choices about how we interact with AI. Companies will keep pushing the envelope, but it's our responsibility to understand the value of our data and protect it.

Own Your Data, Don't Let It Own You

AI is powerful and exciting, but it comes with responsibilities on both sides, yours and the companies creating these systems. You have the power to control your privacy and make sure that you're not giving away more than you're comfortable with. Just because AI can collect data, doesn't mean it should, *or that you have to let it.*

At the end of the day, AI is here to enhance our lives, not take over them. By staying aware of what's being collected and how it's being used, you can keep enjoying the benefits of AI without feeling like you've lost your privacy.

A.I FOR ENTREPRENEURS

This is for all my fellow hustlers, dreamers, and creators who want to take that next big leap and use AI to get there. Let's make this journey fun, accessible, and maybe even game-changing for your entrepreneurial journey. We know entrepreneurship is no walk in the park. It's sleepless nights, juggling responsibilities, and constantly searching for that edge. But what if I told you that AI could be the secret sauce to leveling up your business game, Sounds good, right?

Automating the Grind

There are a lot of tedious, time-consuming tasks that come with running a business. From sorting emails to keeping track of inventory, these things can eat up your time when you should be focusing on the big picture. That's where AI tools shine. Automation is one of the biggest benefits AI offers entrepreneurs, it takes those repetitive tasks off your plate, so you can focus on innovation and growth.

Examples of AI for Automation:

1. **Chatbots for Customer Service:** Tools like **Zendesk** or **Tidio** can handle FAQs, appointment bookings, and even troubleshooting, so you can provide 24/7 customer service without actually being up all night.
2. **Email Marketing with AI:** Programs like **Mailchimp** and **HubSpot** let you automate email campaigns, segment your audience, and track performance, so you can stay connected with your customers and never miss an opportunity.

3. **Inventory and Order Management:** Tools like **TradeGecko** or **Orderhive** automate your inventory tracking, making sure you never run out of stock or miss an order, while keeping your operations smooth.

Know Your Audience, Perfect Your Product

Gone are the days of guessing what your customers want. AI can help you get deep insights into your market and customers with minimal effort.

AI Tools for Market Research:

1. **Google Analytics:** You're probably familiar with this one, but it's worth mentioning. Google Analytics can tell you where your website visitors are coming from, what they're looking for, and how they engage with your site. It's insight your customers' minds.
2. **Crimson Hexagon:** For those who want to dive deeper into social listening and understand brand sentiment, **Crimson Hexagon** uses AI to analyze social media conversations and tell you how people really feel about your products or services.
3. **SurveyMonkey with AI Integration:** Platforms like **SurveyMonkey** can create more intelligent surveys, analyzing responses to give you meaningful insights into customer behavior and preferences.

Make It About Your Customer

Personalization is key when it comes to modern marketing. People want to feel like your product or service was made just for them, and AI can help you create that experience. Imagine having the power to tailor every single interaction based on each specific customer's preferences, without spending hours on it.

AI Tools for Personalization:

1. **Dynamic Pricing with AI:** If you've ever wondered how

Amazon knows exactly when to offer you a discount, that's AI at work. You can use similar AI tools to adjust your pricing based on demand, competition, or customer behavior.

2. **Personalized Product Recommendations:** If you have an e-commerce store, tools like **Yusp** or **Nosto** can analyze what your customers are browsing and buying, then recommend products they're more likely to purchase.

Let the Ideas Flow

This one's for all the content creators out there. Whether you're running a blog, YouTube channel, or social media account, content is king. But let's be real: consistently creating high-quality content can be draining. That's where AI can step in and be your creative partner.

AI Tools for Content Creation:

1. **Jasper (formerly Jarvis):** Need to write blog posts, emails, or social media captions? **Jasper** can generate content ideas, write drafts, and even suggest edits, so you can get more done in less time.
2. **Canva with AI Tools:** Canva is a go-to for designing everything from logos to social media posts. With its AI-powered design suggestions and templates, you can create stunning visuals without being a pro designer.
3. **Lumen5 for Videos:** If video content is more your thing, **Lumen5** turns blog posts into engaging videos using AI, complete with stock footage, music, and voiceovers. Talk about a time-saver!

Marketing with AI

If you're looking to create a marketing campaign using

ChatGPT, first, start by asking ChatGPT to help brainstorm ideas for your campaign. For example, say, "Create a social media campaign for promoting a new pop up event in the town." You'll get tagline ideas, post concepts, and even suggestions for target audiences. Next, you can ask it to help write email newsletters, social media captions, or even outline blog posts to support the campaign. It's all about asking the right questions to get customized, creative strategies!

For Captions:

1. *"Create a catchy Instagram caption for promoting [product/service]."*
2. *"Write an engaging Facebook caption for a [type of business] targeting [audience]."*
3. *"Give me a playful caption for a behind-the-scenes post about [topic]."*
4. *"Can you create a motivating caption for a fitness-related post on Instagram?"*

For Taglines:

1. *"Help me create a memorable tagline for my [business/product]."*
2. *"What's a short, punchy tagline for a brand focused on [values]?"*
3. *"Generate 3 creative taglines for a new AI-based service."*

For Content Ideas:

1. *"Give me 5 content ideas for promoting my [product/business] on Instagram."*
2. *"Can you suggest some interactive content ideas for engaging followers in the [industry] space?"*
3. *"What are some unique content ideas for a TikTok series on*

[topic]?"

For Hashtags and SEO Keywords:

1. *"Generate the best hashtags for a [topic] post targeting [audience]."*
2. *"What are some trending hashtags for promoting a small business in [industry]?"*
3. *"Suggest SEO keywords for ranking high in search results for [topic] on Instagram."*
4. *"Help me create a list of hashtags and SEO keywords for marketing [product/service] to [audience]."*

Tip for Generating Hashtags and SEO Keywords:

Use specific, relevant terms related to your niche and target audience. Combine popular hashtags with a few niche or unique hashtags to reach both broad and targeted audiences. For SEO keywords, focus on relevance, search volume, and user intent, balancing long-tail keywords with high-traffic terms.

Real-World Examples of AI in Action:

Let's look at how some entrepreneurs are already using AI to take their businesses to the next level.

1. **Spotify's Personalized Playlists:** Entrepreneurs in the music industry or app development space can learn from how Spotify uses AI to curate custom playlists for every listener, making each user feel like their experience is one-of-a-kind.
2. **Starbucks' AI-Powered Marketing:** Starbucks uses an AI tool called **Deep Brew** to analyze customer data and predict what each customer will order. This level of personalization has boosted customer loyalty and sales.
3. **AI in Fashion – Stitch Fix:** Stitch Fix uses AI to

recommend outfits based on personal preferences and past purchases. This allows them to offer a tailored shopping experience that keeps customers coming back.
4. **AI in Customer Service – H&M's Virtual Assistant:** H&M uses AI chatbots to answer customer inquiries and make personalized shopping suggestions, creating a seamless and engaging shopping experience.
5. **The Rise of AI in Food Delivery – Domino's Pizza:** Domino's uses an AI-powered voice assistant to take orders over the phone and a predictive analytics tool to estimate delivery times more accurately. This has transformed their customer service experience.

Best Practices for Engaging with AI Tools

Now that you've seen what AI can do, let's talk about how to make the most of it.

1. **Start Small:** Don't try to implement everything at once. Choose one AI tool that addresses a specific need, master it, and then expand.
2. **Stay Curious:** AI is constantly evolving. Keep learning about new features and updates. Subscribe to newsletters, watch tutorials, and join online communities to stay in the loop.
3. **Use Data Wisely:** AI thrives on data, but it's crucial to strike a balance between collecting useful information and respecting your customers' privacy. Be transparent with your audience about what data you're collecting and why.
4. **Test and Iterate:** AI tools are great for experimentation. Test different approaches, whether it's tweaking your pricing strategy or A/B testing email campaigns, and let AI show you what works best.
5. **Human + AI Combo:** The magic happens when you combine your intuition, creativity, and personal touch with the efficiency and intelligence of AI.

AI as Your Entrepreneurial Partner

In the world of entrepreneurship, AI is the business partner who never sleeps, never forgets, and always has your back. It can help you optimize your operations, reach more customers, and personalize your offerings in a way that just wasn't possible before. Whether you're just starting out or scaling up, AI is the toolkit you didn't know you needed but won't be able to live without. So get out there, play with the tools, and let AI help you build the business of your dreams.

A.I IN CAREERS

So, we all want to stay relevant and competitive, right? But let's face it, the professional landscape is changing, and fast. New skills, new tools, and constant innovation can be overwhelming. But instead of seeing AI as a threat to your career, think of it as your secret weapon. A tool you can harness to sharpen your skills, enhance your productivity, and even open up brand-new career opportunities.

Whether you're an accountant, a teacher, a content creator, or even a personal trainer, AI has something to offer. So, let's break it down: how can AI help you level up, no matter where you are in your career?

Get Smarter, Faster

One of the most exciting ways AI is transforming careers is through personalized learning. It's like having a private tutor who's always there, knows your strengths and weaknesses, and can recommend the exact resources you need. You don't have to slog through hours of irrelevant material anymore.

AI Learning Tools:

1. **Coursera & edX (AI-Powered Learning Paths):** These platforms use AI to personalize your learning experience. For example, Coursera can recommend courses based on your career goals, current skills, and even how you learn best. They'll suggest what to take next based on your strengths and weaknesses.
2. **Duolingo (AI-Powered Language Learning):** Learning a new language is one of the most valuable skills

for anyone. Duolingo's AI adapts to how well you're progressing and focuses on the areas you struggle with, making language learning more efficient and engaging.

3. **LinkedIn Learning (Skill Assessment with AI)**: LinkedIn Learning takes a deep dive into your profile and suggests courses that are hyper-relevant to your career path. Plus, you can test your new skills and get certifications to add directly to your resume.

Pro Tip: Instead of passively consuming content, let AI guide you to focus on what will truly enhance your career. Get certified in AI-adjacent skills, even if you're not in a tech field. **Understanding AI is becoming universally valuable.**

Crush Your Workflow

We all know how it feels to be buried under tasks. The good news is AI is a productivity powerhouse. From managing your schedule to automating repetitive tasks, these AI tools will help you get things done with way less stress.

AI Productivity Tools:

1. **Grammarly (AI for Writing and Communication)**: Let's start with one of the basics. Whether you're drafting emails, creating reports, or writing social media posts, **Grammarly** helps make sure your communication is on point. It doesn't just correct spelling and grammar it gives style suggestions, tone adjustments, and even clarity tips.

2. **Notion (AI-Powered Task Management)**: If you're juggling multiple projects or have a to-do list that feels like it's never going to end, **Notion** can help. The platform uses AI to organize your tasks and even suggest better ways to structure your workflow, so you stay focused and productive.

3. **Otter.ai (AI for Meetings and Note-Taking)**: Sick of taking notes during meetings? Let **Otter.ai** do it for

you. This AI tool transcribes conversations in real-time and even highlights key points. Imagine being able to stay fully present in a meeting without worrying about missing important details.

Pro Tip: AI is best used to enhance, not replace, your skills. Use these tools to automate the mundane and free up your brainpower for more strategic, creative work.

Get Ahead of the Competition

Applying for jobs can be exhausting, right? But what if you had AI helping you tailor your resume, prep for interviews, and even search for jobs you didn't even know existed? AI can make the whole process way less tedious, and way more effective.

AI Job Search Tools:

1. **Jobscan (AI Resume Optimization): Jobscan** analyzes job descriptions and matches your resume to highlight the keywords and skills recruiters are looking for. It's like having a personal job application coach telling you exactly how to make your resume stand out.
2. **AI-Powered Mock Interviews:** Platforms like **Interviewing.io** use AI to simulate job interviews based on the roles you're applying for. They even give you feedback on your performance, so you can improve your answers before the real deal.
3. **LinkedIn (AI-Powered Job Suggestions):** LinkedIn uses AI to recommend job openings that match your experience and career goals. It also suggests ways to improve your profile based on the jobs you're interested in, which gives you an edge in a competitive market.

Pro Tip: Use AI to scan job boards, tweak your resume, and prep for interviews, but don't forget that *networking and human connections* still matter. Combine AI's efficiency with your personal touch to stand out.

Future-Proof Your Career

Let's talk about future-proofing. The world is changing, fast, and the jobs of tomorrow might look nothing like today's. That's where AI comes in helping you build skills that will be relevant in the future, not just right now.

AI Tools for Skill Development:

1. **Skillshare (AI-Recommended Creative Classes):** Whether you want to learn photography, graphic design, or something more technical like coding, **Skillshare** uses AI to recommend courses based on your interests and skill level. You can explore creative and business-driven skills that keep you competitive.
2. **AI for Coding – GitHub Copilot:** If you're thinking about learning how to code (or already do), **GitHub Copilot** is a powerful tool. It's an AI that helps write code for you, suggesting snippets based on what you're trying to build.
3. **Trello (AI for Project Management):** Learning how to manage projects and people is another future-proof skill. **Trello** uses AI to suggest project workflows, set deadlines, and keep you organized.

Pro Tip: Don't just focus on "technical" AI skills. Soft skills like leadership, communication, and creativity will be just as important in the future. AI can't replace the human touch, you're still the X factor in your career.

5 Real-World Examples of AI for Career Growth:

1. **Marketing: HubSpot's** AI helps marketers create targeted campaigns and analyze customer behavior, making marketing more data-driven and effective.
2. **Sales: Salesforce Einstein** is an AI assistant that helps sales teams predict which leads are most likely to convert, saving time and boosting results.

3. **Education:** AI-powered platforms like **Khan Academy** are using AI to personalize learning for students, making education more accessible and efficient.
4. **Healthcare:** AI tools like **IBM Watson Health** assist doctors in diagnosing patients more accurately by analyzing huge amounts of medical data.
5. **Freelancing:** If you're a freelancer, AI tools like **Fiverr's Logo Maker** or **Upwork's AI-Powered Matching** help match you with projects that align with your skillset, making it easier to find the right gigs.

AI as Your Career Partner

From learning new skills faster to automating daily tasks, AI empowers you to work smarter, not harder. The key to making the most of AI in your career is to stay open to learning, be willing to experiment, and use AI as a tool that complements your strengths. You've got the creativity, the intuition, and the drive. AI just amplifies all that.

THE FUTURE OF A.I

It's unbelievable but AI is growing fast. It's like we're strapped to a rocket, heading full speed into a future that's equal parts thrilling and unpredictable. So, what does the future of AI look like? Will it take over the world like in sci-fi movies, or will it continue to evolve into something more collaborative, more integrated into our lives? Spoiler: It's more likely the second option. But let's unpack what's next for AI in a way that's a bit rational, and let's leave the "robot uprising" to Hollywood.

AI Gets More Human (Emotional Intelligence)

Right now, AI is already pretty smart, but in the future, it's going to get emotionally smart too. We're not talking about AI shedding a tear while watching a sad movie, but AI that understands human emotions and can respond with empathy. Think about how virtual assistants like Siri or Alexa might evolve. In the future, they won't just set your reminders or play your favorite song, they'll understand if you're stressed, cheer you up, or provide emotional support.

Imagine a world where customer service chatbots aren't just giving you canned responses, but are able to sense frustration in your tone and adjust their approach to help you better. This is where AI and emotional intelligence collide. We're getting to the point where your smart devices might become your best listeners. No judgment, just support.

Personalized Medicine on Steroids

AI in healthcare is going to absolutely transform how we

think about treatment. We're not just talking about using AI to diagnose illnesses faster (though that's already happening); we're talking about AI tailoring medical treatments to your exact genetic makeup. Personalized medicine is set to become a massive industry. Your future doctor might prescribe treatments based on AI analyzing your unique health data, DNA, lifestyle, and history, to give you personalized care that's far more effective than the current one-size-fits-all approach.

We might even see AI-assisted surgeries where robots handle intricate operations with superhuman precision. AI won't replace doctors but will empower them to work faster and with greater accuracy. We're stepping into an era where healthcare becomes proactive instead of reactive. Preventing problems before they even arise? That's the future.

Humans and AI, Side by Side

Now, I know a lot of people worry about AI taking jobs, but here's the truth: AI will take *some* jobs, but it will also create entirely new industries and roles. Think about how computers changed the workforce in the '80s and '90s. Some jobs became obsolete, sure, but new ones popped up that no one had even imagined before. The same will happen with AI.

In the future, AI will handle more of the repetitive, mundane tasks, leaving humans to focus on creativity, problem-solving, and decision-making. Imagine a workplace where your AI assistant handles all the data entry, scheduling, and paperwork, freeing you up to focus on more meaningful, strategic work. In industries like marketing, design, or even law, AI could help analyze trends, spot opportunities, and even draft initial ideas, leaving humans to refine, improve, and implement.

The key here is not to fight against AI but to adapt and use it to enhance what we already do. The future workforce will be one where humans and AI collaborate, making work more efficient and creative.

Autonomous Everything

When we think about the future of AI, we can't skip over autonomous vehicles. AI-powered self-driving cars are just the beginning. The future holds autonomous drones, ships, and even robots that can move and operate independently in industries like agriculture, logistics, and construction.

Imagine this: your pizza being delivered by a drone that navigates to your house without human intervention. Or a farm where AI-powered tractors till the land, plant seeds, and harvest crops with zero human input. Autonomous systems are set to disrupt so many industries, making things faster, safer, and in some cases, cheaper.

But let's take it further. Autonomous factories, where robots and AI systems run entire production lines, only need human intervention for oversight and complex decision-making. It sounds futuristic, but we're not far off.

Fully Immersive Experiences

We've already seen AI influence gaming, music, and even films, but in the future, it's going to create entire entertainment experiences that are tailored to you. Imagine playing a video game where the storyline adapts to your every decision in real time, all thanks to AI that can predict and respond to your choices.

In music, AI might create custom playlists or even write songs that are perfectly in sync with your mood. We've seen AI-generated art, but what about AI-generated movies or TV shows? The future of entertainment will be deeply interactive, with AI helping to create personalized content that changes and evolves based on your preferences and feedback.

The Moral Compass

As AI gets more powerful, so do the ethical questions around it. In the future, there will be an even greater focus on making sure AI is fair, transparent, and doesn't reinforce harmful biases. We'll need strict regulations to ensure that AI is used responsibly, especially as it becomes more integrated into our daily lives.

Imagine a future where every AI system comes with something like a "transparency report" or "ethics certification." This would show you exactly how the AI operates, what data it's using, and who is behind the technology. This level of transparency will be critical as AI continues to shape society. We'll need to hold developers accountable to ensure AI is used for good.

A Greener Planet

Finally, AI is going to play a huge role in tackling some of the world's biggest challenges, like climate change. From optimizing energy grids to improving waste management, AI can help us live more sustainably. In the future, we might see AI helping cities reduce energy consumption by adjusting lighting, heating, and cooling systems in real-time, based on data like weather forecasts and current usage patterns.

AI can also help predict environmental disasters and offer solutions before they happen. We can imagine a world where we can use AI to track pollution levels, anticipate floods, or even help restore ecosystems. We're talking about AI as a force for good, helping us protect our planet and create a more sustainable future.

The Future is Bright

So, what's next for AI? It's AI evolving into a tool that enhances our lives, our work, and our planet more so than it is now. From smarter healthcare to autonomous systems, immersive entertainment, and sustainable living, the future of AI is brimming with possibility.

The key to all of this is staying open to what's coming. AI isn't something to fear. Instead, it's a technology that we can guide and shape for the better. As long as we keep ethical considerations in mind, the future of AI looks like a bright, collaborative, and innovative space.

THE AI JOURNEY IS JUST BEGINNING

By now, you've got a pretty solid grasp of what AI is and how it can fit into your life. We've taken a look at everything from using AI to boost your creativity, to leveraging it for self-care, to even helping you build and run a business. The goal here wasn't just to give you a bunch of facts about AI, it was to show you how it's evolving into a tool you can use every single day.

The truth is, that AI is going to keep growing, adapting, and becoming a bigger part of our lives. And that's not something to fear, but something to embrace. The more you understand it, the more empowered you'll be to use AI to your advantage, whether that's to streamline your work, enhance your mental wellness, or tap into new creative possibilities.

And at the very end of the day, AI isn't here to replace us, it's here to help us. And the sooner we get comfortable with it, the better equipped we'll be to navigate the exciting (and sometimes challenging) world ahead.

So, keep experimenting, keep learning, and most of all, keep an open mind. You've got this, and with AI by your side, the possibilities are endless. With that, I want to thank you for letting me guide you on this journey you've begun. We've covered a lot, but there's so much more to discover. Stay curious, stay engaged, and welcome to your AI-empowered future!

ACKNOWLEDGMENTS

I would like to extend my gratitude for choosing this book and taking the time to dive into its pages. It is a deep passion of mine to learn topics outside my usual wheelhouse and making them easy to understand for everyone. This is my very first published book, and I would love to hear your thoughts, recommendations, and even what you'd like to "**Master'** next! Leave a comment or follow me on any social platform @waskeyra. Your support means the world to me, and I can't wait to write for you again. Here's to more learning, growing, and mastering together!

ABOUT THE AUTHOR

Sonyque Suriel

Sonyque Suriel is a passionate learner with a knack for simplifying complex topics. With a love for exploring subjects outside her wheelhouse, she created Mastering AI: A Guide to Understanding and Growing with AI and GPT to make Artificial Intelligence accessible to everyday people.

As a Caribbean American from Antigua, she brings a fresh, approachable perspective to the world of AI, empowering readers to embrace technology without intimidation. When she's not writing, she's traveling, exploring new cultures, or diving into her next learning adventure.

@waskeyra

www.ingramcontent.com/pod-product-compliance
Lightning Source LLC
Chambersburg PA
CBHW030050230526
45471CB00003B/1033